CHRISTMAS ARRANGEMENTS

by Mary Gudgeon and John Clowes

Christmas Arrangements

MARY GUDGEON
& JOHN CLOWES

M & J PUBLICATIONS

Contents

First published in Great Britain in 1984 by
M & J Publications, The Hollies, Cattlegate Road,
Crews Hill, Enfield, Middx, England EN2 9DW (0992) 461895

Reprinted 1986

Production Services by Book Production Consultants,
Cambridge. Printed and bound in England by
Hazell Watson & Viney Ltd, Aylesbury, Bucks.

ISBN 0 9509748 0 3

Arrangements by Mary Gudgeon, John Clowes and Wendy Smith
© Copyright John Clowes 1984

Introduction

With this colourful and imaginative book anyone can fill their home with glittering and individual decorations easily and economically. All the traditional favourites have been included as well as some ideas which may be new to you. Whether you are an experienced arranger or just a beginner you will find arrangements which should inspire you to action.

The flowers and foliage we have used are artificial and the bases and containers are purposely simple. In this way we have avoided fresh flowers, which are expensive in winter, and we have shunned unusual containers which may be beautiful to photograph, but are impossible to imitate.

This simplicity of approach will hopefully tempt more and more people to try this fascinating art. Just one trip to your local garden centre, department store or large florist should see you with everything you need.

For each arrangement throughout the book you will find a list of the materials we have used. This is followed by step-by-step instructions on how the same effect can be re-created. Simple line drawings illustrate the starting points, the scale and the key steps to follow. On separate pages you will find detailed instructions and diagrams on how to wire stems, tie ribbons, prepare candles and finish off the back of the arrangement.

If you are an expert on flower arranging you will know that all the ideas pictured can be varied and adapted to great effect. We have given suggestions on suitable variations which will create a different look to each of them.

Remember that whatever arrangements you make this year will also be an investment for the future. Store them in plastic bags in the loft and they can be brought out year after year. They will add sparkle, excitement and your own touch of luxury to the festive season.

The equipment you will need

You don't need a mountain of equipment to make flower arrangements with artificial material, but some things like an efficient pair of wire cutters will make life easier.

Wire Cutters

You can use a pair of pliers borrowed from the DIY kit or buy a handy pair of wire cutters specially produced for florist work. You will need them to cut stems to length as well as to trim wires evenly. Florist scissors often have a special notch which is suitable for cutting thin wire.

Wire

Stub wires are useful for adding stems to baubles, cones and foliage pieces. They are available in various lengths and thicknesses. A small packet of two different gauges will be enough to start with.

Useful Extras

Scissors for trimming foliage and cutting ribbon. *Knife* for cutting blocks of oasis and curling ribbon. *Aluminium Foil* for covering plasticine bases. *Stemwrap* for covering the wire stems of material to give a natural green colour.

The mechanics you should understand

The word 'mechanics' is used in flower arranging circles to describe the devices which are used to hold flower and foliage stems in position.

The green plastic foam pieces which absorb water and are used as a base for fresh flowers are well known. However, the brown plastic foam pieces and the various types of clay material used for dried and artificial material may be new to you. Your local garden centre will be sure to have some of them available.

Green Plastic Foam

Use only with fresh material or when the shape, like the circle bases, are particularly convenient.

Brown Plastic Foam

Various shapes are available in this material from block, to ball and cones.

Plasticine or 'Stay Soft'

This type of material which will not set solid is essential when you are positioning candles which will need to be replaced after they have been burned.

Dri-Hard

This material will set solid after about 12 hours and is useful to create a permanent arrangement.

Plasticine Anchors

This tiny four-pronged anchor is used to hold the mechanics (foam block, plasticine or Dri-Hard) in a container so that they do not slip or fall over when you have completed the arrangement. One anchor is usually sufficient for most arrangements but more may be needed if you have a long sausage-shaped base or a large block to hold steady.

Oasis fix

A fixative material is needed to secure the plasticine anchor to the container of your choice. Oasis fix is a brand name for one of these fixatives, but others are just as suitable.

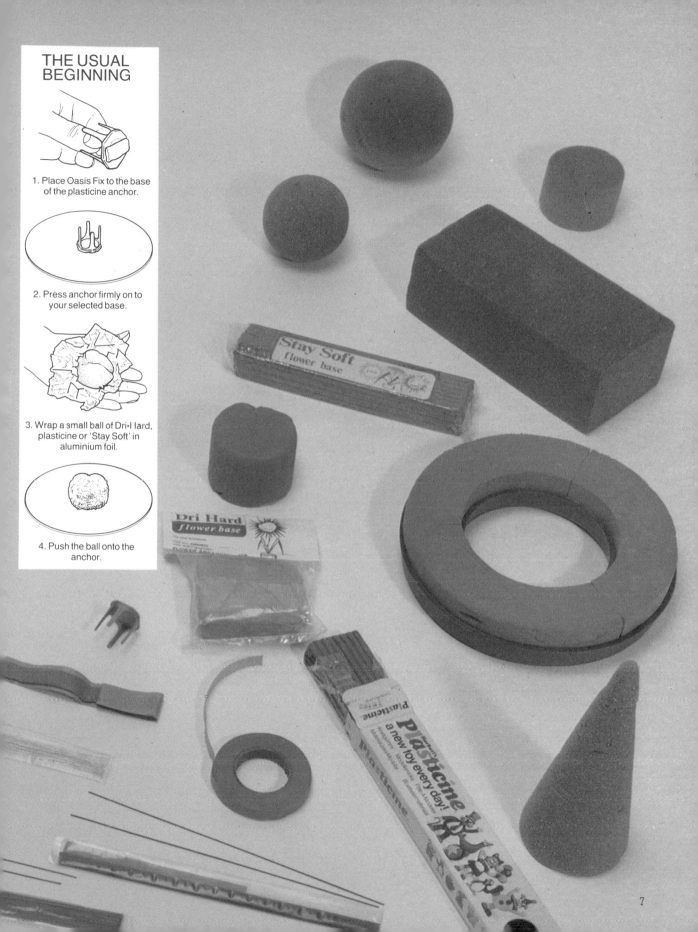

Stay Soft
flower base

Dri Hard
flower base

Plasticine
a new toy every day!

The bases you can find

In this book we have used simple bases and containers which you can buy easily and cheaply. If you own more elaborate containers by all means use them, remembering that the balance between an arrangement and its container is important.

Wood Slices

These are available in various sizes which can be bought either with a polished surface or a rough one. Remember to check the underside for roughness before placing these bases on a polished surface.

Cake Bases

Very useful and cheap when you are planning to hide the base completely with material.

Bark

Pieces of bark are available in various sizes. It is light, full of texture and re-useable. If you make small holes in the bark you can wire on a piece of Dri-Hard or foam – securing it from below.

Scroll Bases

Black is the most commonly found colour in various sizes.

Wire Shapes

Circular wire bases are useful when producing the traditional round decoration for the front door. Sphagnum moss is first wired onto the circle to give a base through which you can push the stems.

Specially Shaped Bases

The sleigh pictured here is typical of the various types of bases which can be found. Although not available everywhere, your local garden centre or florist may be able to help.

The containers which are useful

A small collection of the different types of containers will not cost you a fortune nor be difficult to find. You can use home-made lids instead of plastic saucers and painted plastic bottles instead of vases.

Saucers

White, black and beige saucers are available, some of which are designed to take the standard size plastic foam cylinder.

Candlesticks

Silver may be super, but plastic is cheaper.
The only thing to consider is to make sure the base is large enough to keep it stable.

Candle Cups

These specially shaped cups fit into the top of a candlestick or wine bottle and have a large enough container to take a plastic foam cylinder or hold an amount of plasticine.

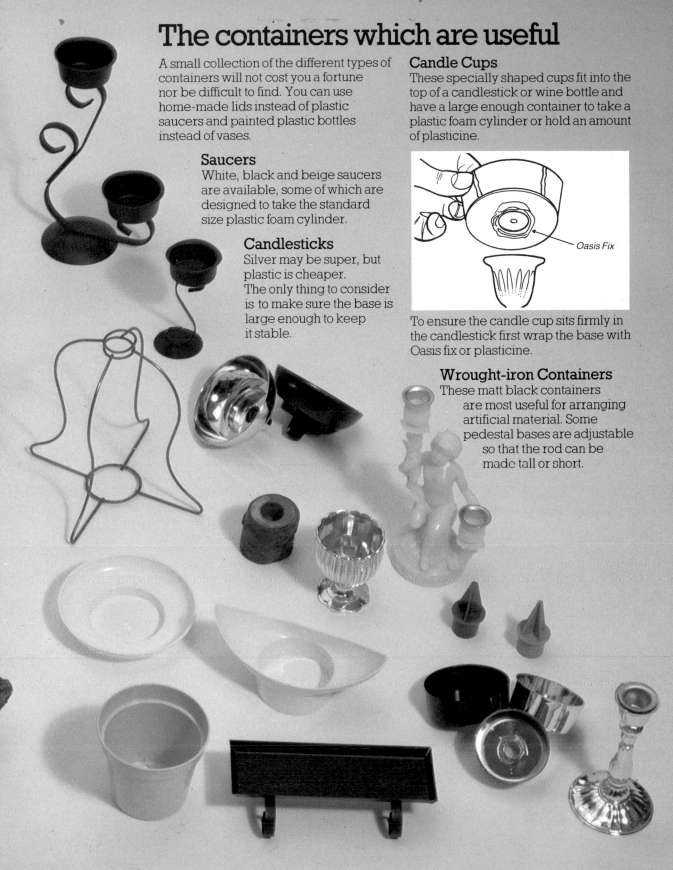

Oasis Fix

To ensure the candle cup sits firmly in the candlestick first wrap the base with Oasis fix or plasticine.

Wrought-iron Containers

These matt black containers are most useful for arranging artificial material. Some pedestal bases are adjustable so that the rod can be made tall or short.

The materials for arranging

Foliage

Artificial foliage material is available in many different forms. The traditional evergreen leaves of holly, pine, fir and ivy are the favourite choices, but this is by no means an exhaustive list. The attractive shape of fern leaves, and the bushy boldness of ruscus are popular. Material which comes complete with berries in the correct scale, like mistletoe and holly is most useful.

All material is available in natural shades of green and most is also available in gold, silver, white and red-flocked. There is also an abundance of glittered leaves and pine needles.

Some of the foliage material used in the arrangements in this book are only available in large branches. Where this is so, we have cut this down into smaller pieces and added a wire stem to each piece. Usually one large branch has been sufficient for one arrangement. Remember when selecting foliage that the leaves should be in scale to the final arrangement.

An aerosol can of gold or silver paint can transform dried material and natural seed heads such as teasels and beech nut cases into very useful material for Christmas arrangements.

Flowers

At Christmas time the most appropriate flowers to use in arrangements are carnations, poinsettias, roses and Christmas roses. These artificial flowers are available in many different forms, colours and sizes.

Small plastic flowers are inexpensive and indestructible. The same thing made from polyester material (known generally as 'silks') are more delicate, but equally as long lasting. Whatever the price, the flowers you buy this year are also an investment for the future. You can store the arrangement away until next year or re-use the material in a new way each year.

The festive colours red, gold, silver and white are most often associated with Christmas decorations, but there is no reason why any colour should not be used. When you have chosen the flowers make sure that you have a contrast of textures when put against the chosen foliage.

Accessories

Baubles, bangles and bright berries will add interesting highlights to each arrangement. Glass baubles which already have a wire stem attached are easiest to use or you can add a wire stem to the traditional tree-hanging type.

Artificial fruit can also add some unusual colour and shapes. There are limes, lemons, strawberries, oranges and plenty of others. Look out for tiny toadstool replicas which add an authentic look to a woodland scene on a bark or tree slice base.

Bird figures, complete with feathers can be useful to lift an arrangement out of the ordinary. Plump robins are favourite, followed by colourful ducks and other garden birds.

Nuts, cones and seed heads are useful to add interesting texture to your decorations. Poppy heads should first be sprayed with gold or silver paint, but fir cones are best left natural or just the ends tipped with white emulsion paint or spray snow to give the impression of a winter's scene. Fixing a wire into a walnut shell is possible with a hot needle but you can buy these already prepared with a wire stem.

The technique of wiring

With most artificial material you will frequently need to lengthen a stem or add a completely new one. Using florist wire and covering it with a green stem-binding tape is the easiest and firmest way. A wire stem allows the arranger to position the flower or leaf in exactly the right spot. Some wires are pictured on Page 6.

Different thicknesses (gauges) of wire are available from very fine 'silver' reel wire to chunky, short stem wires. The general rule is to use the thinnest wire which is just sufficiently strong to do the job required. In this way your arrangement will not lose its natural look and become too rigid.

HOW TO ADD A STEM

1 Bend a stub wire in half and place the bend over the existing stem.

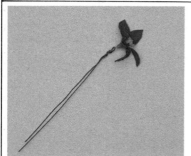

2 Twist one of the wire ends (called a 'leg') firmly around the stem and the other wire.

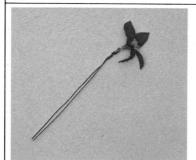

3 Use wire cutters to cut the ends to the required length.

4 Wrap wires with stem-binding tape.

HOW TO WIRE A LEAF

1 Work on the back of the leaf and stitch a wire through the centre of the leaf.

2 Bend both the wires down towards the base of the leaf.

3 Twist one wire 'leg' tightly around the stem and the other wire.

4 Wrap wires with stem-binding tape.

Shatterproof and plastic baubles are sturdy and you can wire these as you would a foliage stem. With delicate glass baubles you may break the decoration if the wire is twisted tightly around the protruding end. Instead, use the metal hanging loop to attach the wire which is made firm with stem-binding tape.

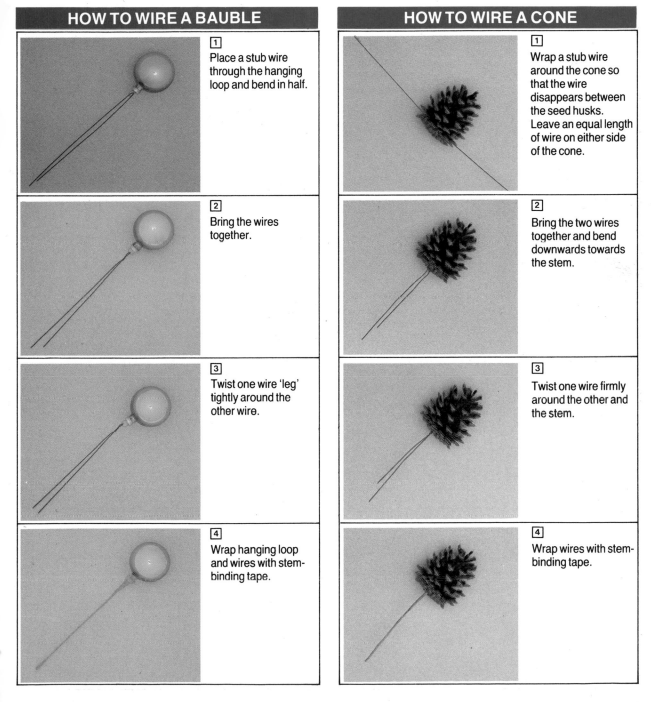

HOW TO WIRE A BAUBLE

1
Place a stub wire through the hanging loop and bend in half.

2
Bring the wires together.

3
Twist one wire 'leg' tightly around the other wire.

4
Wrap hanging loop and wires with stem-binding tape.

HOW TO WIRE A CONE

1
Wrap a stub wire around the cone so that the wire disappears between the seed husks. Leave an equal length of wire on either side of the cone.

2
Bring the two wires together and bend downwards towards the stem.

3
Twist one wire firmly around the other and the stem.

4
Wrap wires with stem-binding tape.

Candles

Candles have a vital role to play in Christmas arrangements. They add a festive glow to a table centre or mantlepiece arrangement.

It is important that the candles are easily replaceable so that the line of the decoration is not ruined and new candles can be re-lit on another evening.

To achieve this, use plasticine or 'Stay-Soft' as your base material or a block of plastic foam. Prepare the candle with cocktail sticks before it is positioned in an arrangement. This technique means that the candle can be more easily positioned vertically.

There are many candles available nowadays of all shapes, sizes and colours. Here we have illustrated some of the types which you will find in department stores and garden centres from early autumn onwards. Red is the most popular colour, although silver and golden candles are stocked in large numbers.

When selecting a candle for use in an arrangement, bear in mind that once lit the flame will gradually creep lower and lower. If you light the candle it must be extinguished before it reaches the flowers or foliage, especially if they are polyester or plastic. It is also worth considering that the thicker the candle the slower it will burn. It is wise therefore to choose the thickest candle possible which remains in proportion to the rest of the arrangement.

When positioning candles, make sure that they are straight and perfectly vertical from all angles. A slight tilt will become most irritating at a later date.

When you use several candles in an arrangement make sure that they are not all the same height. Simply buy candles of different lengths or buy them all the longest required and cut some down to size with a knife.

Candlesticks

Creating a flower arrangement on the top of a candlestick is popular. Buy a special candle cup in a colour to match the base and fit into the candlestick using Oasis fix.

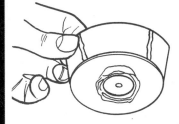

Wrap Oasis fix around the base of the cup.

Push firmly into the top of the candlestick.

Fit a plasticine anchor inside the candle cup.

Push a circular piece of plastic foam into the cup or a ball of plasticine onto the anchor.

Preparing candles

Break two cocktail sticks in half and tape the four pieces to the base of the candle.

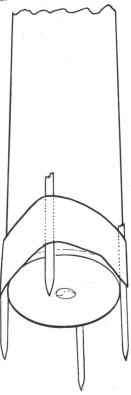

Candle Holders

Small plastic holders are available for a few pence which hold a candle firmly and push easily into plastic foam.

Some of the ribbons available

Tying Ribbons

Many people find that tying ribbons and bows to make them look pretty is a difficult job. However with a little practice and the following step-by-step instructions everyone should be able to add a crisp bow to their arrangements without trouble.

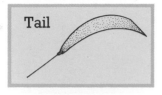

Tail

This ribbon piece is simply a length of ribbon which has been pinched together at one end with a double leg wire added.

1. Bend a stub wire in half.

2. Pinch the end 1 inch of ribbon together and place the bend of wire onto the ribbon.

3. Twist one wire leg around the ribbon and the other wire to firmly trap the ribbon and produce a sturdy stem.

4. Use wire cutters to trim ends evenly. Wrap wires with stem-binding tape.

Single Loop

This is the most versatile of ribbon pieces. It can be used singly or can be positioned with stems pointing towards each other to give the impression of a figure of eight bow.

1. Hold the ribbon to make one loop and a tail to the required length.

2. Pinch the end of the loop firmly together and hold. Then cut the remaining ribbon from the roll.

3. Bend a stub wire in half and place the bend over the pinched end of the ribbon.

4. Twist as tightly as possible and wire leg around the pinched part of the ribbon and the other length of wire.

5. Twist several times to trap the ribbon and produce a sturdy stem.

6. Cut wires to required length.

7. Wrap wires with stem-binding tape.

8. Pull the loop into shape.

Double Loop

A useful ribbon piece for the experienced arranger.

1. Hold the ribbon to make two loops and a tail to the required length.

2. Follow steps 2-8 as shown in the Single Loop instructions.

Triple Loop

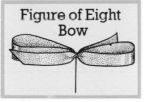

For bigger and bold arrangements this larger bow is most useful.

1. Hold the ribbon to make three loops and a tail to the required length.

2. Follow steps 2-8 as shown in the Single Loop instructions.

Figure of Eight Bow

Illustrated below is the easiest way for the inexperienced to tie a figure of eight bow. A professional will pinch the ribbon together at each stage, but this needs practice.

1. Fold the ribbon to the required size so that you have three layers.

2. Cut off the remaining ribbon.

3. Pinch the centre of the ribbon together tightly.

4. Twist a fine silver wire firmly around the pinched ribbon.

5. Twist one wire leg around the other a couple of times.

6. Pull the loops into shape.

The shapes to follow

The traditional arrangement will be more pleasing to the eye if it fits into one of the 'basic shapes' which flower arrangers find so useful.

If you can keep your material within one of the outlines shown here you should end up with good proportions, line and balance.

All arrangements should have a height which balances its width and you should choose material which naturally falls easily into the shape you have chosen.

If you are a beginner the 'Symmetrical Triangle' or the 'Circular All-Round' shapes are the easiest to master. After you feel more confident, the curved outlines are well worth attempting.

These suggested shapes are presented to help, but not to restrict your own creativity. If you achieve a shape which is pleasing but doesn't fall within these guidelines so well and good. Remember that your arrangement is there to please you and your family – beauty is in the eye of the beholder.

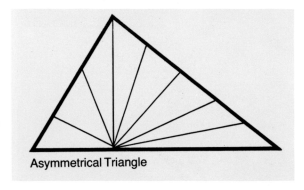
Asymmetrical Triangle

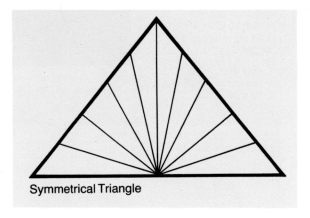
Symmetrical Triangle

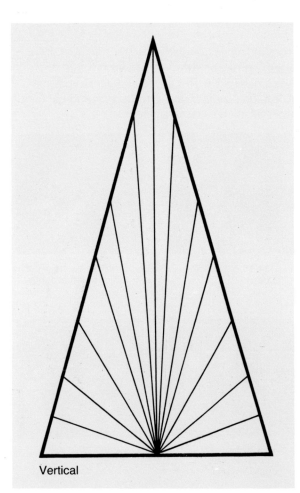
Vertical

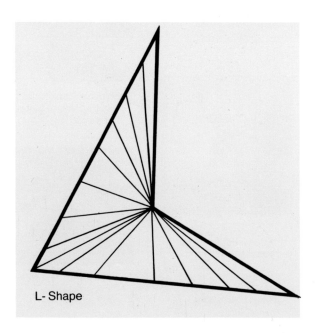
L- Shape

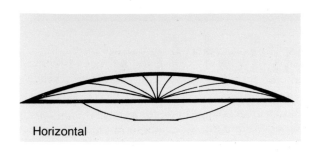

Horizontal

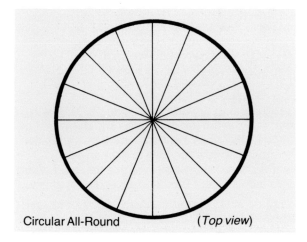

Circular All-Round   (*Top view*)

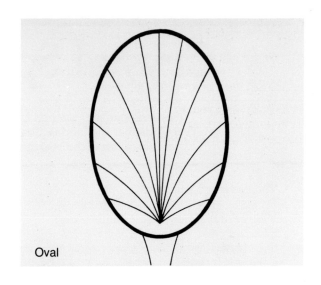

Oval

Upright Crescent

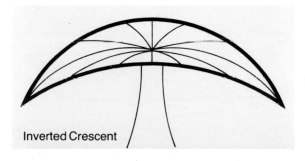

Inverted Crescent

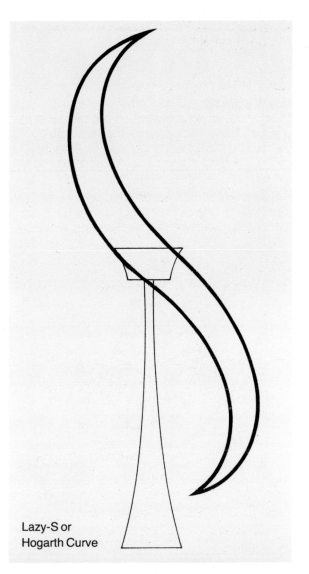

Lazy-S or
Hogarth Curve

21

Crystal Spangled Tree

The arrangement pictured here makes an unusual substitute for a
real Christmas tree and is ideal where space is limited. It captures all
the glitter of the real thing, but on a much smaller scale.

The items you will need
3 Sprays white glittered conifer foliage
1 Piece of bark (approx. 12 inches long)
5 Red apples
5 Red baubles
2 Father Christmas figures
2 Small red crackers
1 Red star
3 Red bells
2 Yards red ribbon
Plasticine anchor
Dri-Hard, Oasis fix, Aluminium foil

How it is made

First create an attractive tree using the white
conifer foliage. Stick a plasticine anchor in
the middle of the bark with Oasis fix. Now wrap a
ball of Dri-Hard in aluminium foil and push onto
the anchor.

Follow the plan to make the first three points of the
tree (Fig. 1). The central piece should be about 14
inches tall. Complete the bushy shape, making

sure the front pieces come forward and overlap
the bark (Fig. 2). If there is any material over use
this to fill in at the back to camouflage the stems.

Start the decoration of the tree with the five red
apples. Wires can easily be pushed into the stem
ends of the apples and the wires cut to length.
Keep the apples at the bottom half of the
arrangement to provide visual weight. Now wire
the red star at the top of the tree and then use fine
wire to fix the bells, baubles, crackers and Father
Christmas's around the tree to give an even
covering. It is usually better to see that everything
points in a different direction and nothing touches.

Complete with several 'figure-of-eight' bows (see
Page 19 for details). In the arrangement we have
used three at the front and two at the back.
Increase the number if you think this is needed for
your arrangement, but don't overcrowd.

 Variations
*Use green pine foliage to create the tree and
then provide the glitter with various pieces
of decoration in gold.*

Fig. 1

Fig.2

Red & Gold Slice

This simple, yet stunning decoration is ideal for an occasional table. It uses an inexpensive wood slice as a base which is contrasted with the delicate red ribbon.

The items you will need
Small wood slice
1 Red candle
2 Stems of gold covered fir foliage
5 Red baubles
1 Yard red decorette ribbon
Plasticine anchor
Oasis fix, Plasticine, Aluminium foil

How it is made
Use Oasis fix to stick the plasticine anchor in the centre of the wood slice. Cover a small ball of plasticine with aluminium foil and push onto the anchor.

Prepare the candle with cocktail sticks taped to the base as shown on Page 15 and position vertically (Fig. 1). Pull off separate branches from the stem of gold fir and wire each piece separately. You should have approximately 14 pieces. Use them to radiate from a position at the base of the candle (Fig. 2). Repeat the same process at the back.

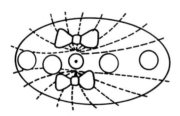

Now wire the red baubles and position in a similar way between the front and back sections of the arrangement. Make two triple-loop bows, as shown on Page 19 and position these front and back in the centre of the radiating gold fir.

 Variations
Try a pink candle and matching baubles in contrast to silver fir foliage to create the same shape, but a different mood.

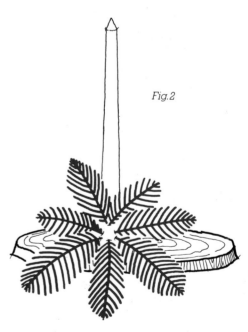

Fig.2

Byzantine Cone

A traditional design used for centuries as a Christmas display.
It looks particularly effective in a hallway as an attractive greeting for
your guests.

The items you will need

The materials we have used in this arrangement can be
bought at florists or garden centres. This however, can
be rather expensive but you can substitute various
items which can be collected free. In the summer
collect small seed heads of poppy and echinops. In the
autumn collect acorns and wire whilst green. They can
all be sprayed various colours before arranging.

Our choice

Miniature artificial fruits (apples, pears, limes)	Holly
Green fir	Golden vase
Mini-fir cones	Optional red base
Mistletoe leaves	Foam cone for artificial flowers
Giant red glixia heads	Dri-Hard, Cane

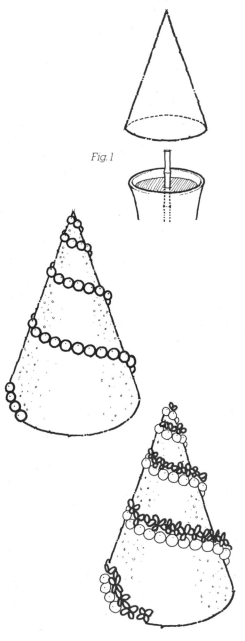

Fig.1

How it is made

Each piece must be wired separately and the stem cut to
approximately ½ inch long (see photograph). Fill the vase
with Dri-Hard and position a thin short cane so that it is
central, vertical and sticks up about 2 inches above the rim of
the vase. When set, push the foam cone centrally onto the
cane (Fig. 1).

Start at the top and create a helter skelter spiral down and
around the cone using one type of material. Choose a
contrasting material for the next spiral and keep everything
close together. Continue in this way until the cone is
covered.

 Variations

*Use poppy heads and acorns sprayed various colours.
You can also try to make an all-gold or all-silver
Byzantine Cone.*

Festive Table Centre

No Christmas table is worthy of the name without a suitable decoration. For evening dinners this circular arrangement with candles is low enough to allow conversation plus the added glow of soft candlelight.

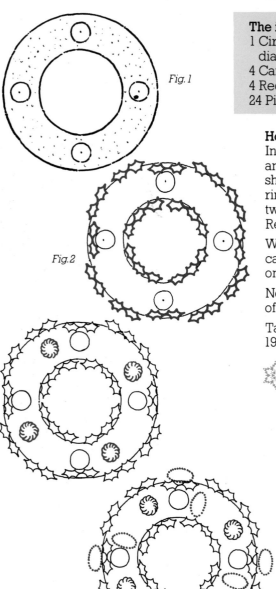

Fig. 1

Fig. 2

The items you will need

1 Circular Oasis holder 12 inches diameter
4 Candle holders
4 Red candles
24 Pieces of holly with berries
8 Christmas roses
8 Silver bells
4 Snow-tipped fir cones
3 Yards red ribbon

How it is made

Inset candles in their holders and push in at exactly 12, 3, 6 and 9 o'clock positions (Fig. 1). Cut the pieces of holly very short and wire each berried piece. Cover the outside of the ring with holly – one piece on the outside of the candle and two pieces on the outside edge between the candles (Fig. 2). Repeat on the inside of the ring.

Wire the pine cones and place on top of the ring between candles. A Christmas rose goes to the left of each candle and one below each candle on the outside of the ring.

Now wire the silver bells in pairs and position between each of the pine cones and Christmas rose.

Take the ribbon and make eight triple-loop bows (see Page 19) and position one each side of the candles.

Variations

White spiral candles can be used as a substitute for the red candles. The circular oasis holders are available in several sizes. If you use a larger base you will need extra pieces of holly and some more red ribbon to fill between the four candles.

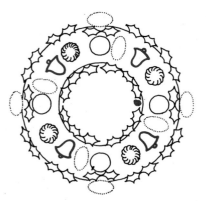

Bell & Robin

This arrangement has everything that is traditionally part of a
Christmas arrangement . . . robin . . . bell . . . holly . . . twigs . . . fir branches.
It is best displayed against a plain background so that the
line of the branches can be seen easily.

The items you will need
Long wood slice
Twigs from the garden or hedgerow
2 Stems short-needled pine
7 Stems holly with berries
Golden bell
3 Fir cones
1 Robin
Nesting material
Plasticine anchor
Oasis fix, Dri-Hard, Aluminium foil

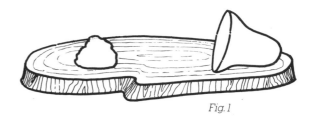

Fig. 1

How it is made

Position the bell at one end of the wooden slice
and keep it in position with a small piece of Oasis
fix. Position the plasticine anchor one third the
way from the other end with Oasis fix and top
with a ball of Dri-Hard covered in
aluminium foil (Fig. 1).

Find some twigs with interesting shapes and cut
to length to give three points of your basic triangle
(Fig. 2). Now complete the shape with twigs at points 4, 5, 6 and 7.

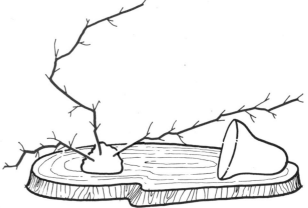

Fig. 2

Cut the pine needle sprays down to three-headed pieces
and secure each piece with a double-leg wire. Push in the
pine foliage to form a tight circle using about seven pieces.
Next add colour with the holly berries and leaves whose
stems will need cutting to length.

Wire the three snow-tipped fir cones and position to
visually balance your triangle. Fill in the back of the
arrangement with pine spray foliage and holly leaves.

Complete the arrangement with a robin either on the
slice looking into the bell, or perched on the top lip of the
bell. Add some nesting material to the inside of the bell.

 Variations
*Instead of the bell try an ordinary
plant pot but spray one side with
snow to give it life.*

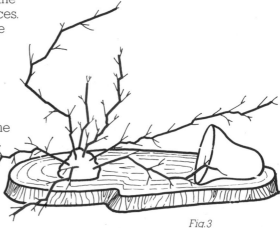

Fig. 3

31

Perfect Present

Ribbon bows add much to a gift, but a miniature arrangement on a plainly wrapped present could well bring as much admiration and thanks as the contents.

The items you will need
1 Red carnation
1 Bunch of red glixia flowers
2 Miniature white carnations
4 Pieces of holly
1 Stem of silver skeletonized leaves
1 Yard red ribbon
Oasis fix, Plasticine, Aluminium foil

How it is made
This dainty arrangement will be studied very closely by the recipient so you must work tidily. Where pieces are wired, the wire should be covered with a green tape called 'Stem Wrap'.

The base of this arrangement is a piece of plasticine 1 inch square by ½ inch deep, wrapped in aluminium foil.

Cut two triple-leaf pieces from the silver skeletonized spray each with a short (½ inch) stem. Position these at opposite ends (Fig. 1). On the other sides of the square, position a single skeletonized leaf.

Wire each holly piece with a short double-leg wire and push the holly into the four corners of the plasticine.

Now wire and stem wrap the white mini-carnations and position at points as shown in Figure 2.

Two more skeletonized leaves are wired, and positioned pointing slightly upwards over the carnation stems (Fig. 3). Now cut the stem of the red carnation so that it will sit right on the top of the plasticine.

Make two triple-loop bows as shown on Page 19 and cover wires with stem wrap. Shorten the stems so that the ribbon fits right up to the plasticine on each side.

Fill in with tiny glixia flowers keeping inside the outline of the arrangement.

A tiny piece of Oasis fix will stick the arrangement to the gift wrapping.

Variations
Start by deciding on the wrapping paper and select your material to suit. For a gift wrapped in red paper try green fir foliage instead of the silver skeletonized leaves plus white silk flowers and silver ribbon.

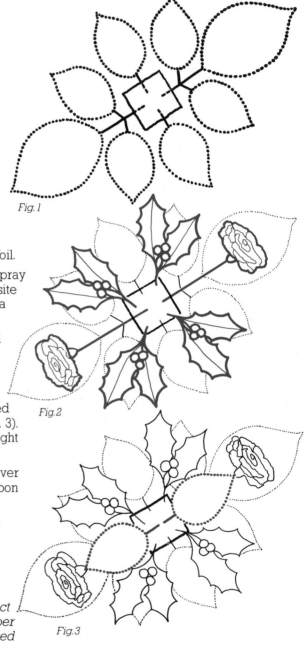

Fig. 1

Fig. 2

Fig. 3

Exploding Cracker

Normal crackers are a short-lived teatime treat. Now here is a way to capture the exciting explosion and illustrate the flying contents which are shown radiating from the centre of this arrangement.

The items you will need
1 Oblong silver cake base
1 White and gold cracker
2 Stems of silver fern
5 Stems of silver skeletonized leaves
5 Silver icicles
5 Gold flowers
5 Gold parcels on stems
3 Yards gold gift tie
Plasticine anchor
Oasis fix, Dri-Hard, Aluminium foil

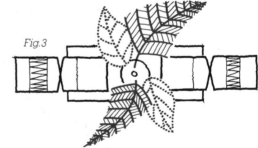

Fig. 1

Fig. 2

How it is made

First cut the cracker in half and use Oasis fix or glue to stick the ends to the cake base. Position the plasticine anchor in the centre of the cracker with Oasis fix and push a small ball of Dri-Hard covered in aluminium foil onto the prongs (Fig. 1).

Start with a silver icicle in the centre and cut to length so that it is about half the width of the cracker (Fig. 2). To achieve the width of the arrangement use silver plated fern to overlap the board by about 2 inches (Fig. 3).

Gradually fill in the centre with silver leaves and icicles making sure all the pieces radiate from a single point. Fill in with gold flowers and gold parcels cut shorter than the surrounding leaves.

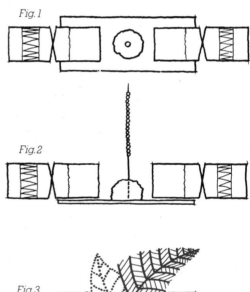

Fig. 3

Finish off with pieces of gold tie. Make 5 loops with gift tie and position in the centre. Single strands of this gold tie are wired and pushed into position to fill in and give the impression of an explosion.

 Variations
A red and white cracker using silver foliage and red glittered flowers is an attractive alternative.

I Saw Three Ships

An illustration of one of the country's favourite Carols proves an eye-catching novelty.

The items you will need
3 White boat-shaped containers
3 Large silver glittered leaves for sails
7 Stems of holly with berries
15 Blue baubles
9 Silver baubles
24 Silver rose leaves
3 Sticks for masts
½ Yard blue ribbon
3 Plasticine anchors
Oasis fix, Dri-Hard, Aluminium foil

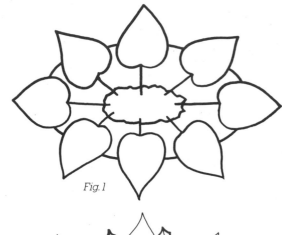

Fig. 1

How it is made
Use Oasis fix to position a plasticine anchor in the centre of a boat-shaped container. Cover a ball of Dri-Hard with aluminium foil and push onto the anchor.

Take silver rose leaves and overlap the edges of the container (Fig. 1). Each stem of holly is broken down into five sprigs and a double-leg wire fixed to each. Position around the rim of the boat between the rose leaves (Fig. 2).

Now wire each bauble and use 5 blue and 3 silver to fill the container. Fill in between the baubles with holly stems and rose leaves.

To make the sail push the top of the stick through the large silver leaf and wire into position. Now bend the leaf as shown in Figure 3, and wire the bottom of the leaf so that it retains the curve.

Glue the ribbon onto the top of the mast and cut a V-shape to make into a flag. Push the whole sail into centre of the boat making sure that the mast is vertical.

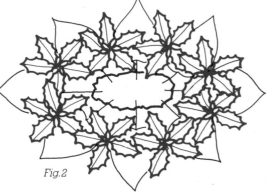

Fig. 2

❄ Variations
Children may like to paint multi-coloured sails made and cut from stiff white cardboard to give an oriental touch.

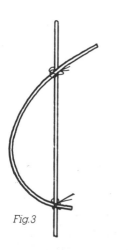

Fig. 3

Three Candle Mantel

This joyous riot of colour needs extra care in placement if it is not to look a jumble. You can use any material left over after decorating the Christmas tree.

The items you will need

3 Red candles	5 Pieces of holly
1 Rectangular cake base	1 Piece red skeletonized leaf
1 Large silver bauble	1 Red parcel
2 Medium red baubles	1 Piece green pine foliage
1 Small gold bauble	2 Yards gold decorette ribbon
3 Pine cones	2 Plasticine anchors
1 Stem silver boxwood	Oasis fix, Plasticine
2 Stems gold fir foliage	

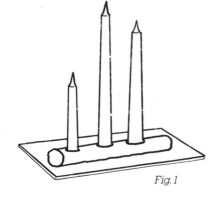

Fig. 1

How it is made

Position the two plasticine anchors to the left and right of the board using Oasis fix. Make a sausage shape with plasticine and push onto the anchors.

Cut the candles to length and tape cocktail sticks to the base of each. Position the tallest candle in the centre and use the other two on either side (Fig. 1). Cut green pine foliage to length and use to hide the plasticine around the base (Fig. 2). Now wire the large silver bauble and two medium size red baubles and position at base level just overhanging the cake base. Fill in between with green pine foliage, fir cones and silver boxwood.

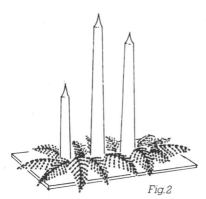

Fig. 2

Now wire the two small baubles and position at the face of the arrangement on different levels (Fig. 3). Position the last pine cone in front of the middle candle and use silver boxwood and the red skeletonized leaf material to fill in. Position holly around the candle bases and display the red parcel attractively.

Gold material now adds the final touches to the arrangement. Use gold covered fir to complete the shape and golden bows to add lightness. A triple-loop bow is positioned between the shortest and tallest candle and two triple-loop bows are set at the front.

Use any material over to fill in at the back.

 Variations
Make sure that whatever colour of candle you choose, you pick out the same colour with some of the baubles.

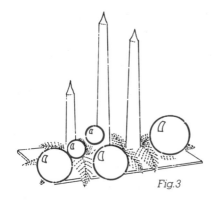

Fig. 3

Snow Ring

This versatile arrangement can be used all round the home to great effect. Try a fireplace, table centre, a coffee table or sideboard.

The items you will need
1 Round silver cake board
1 Stem of white pine foliage
3 Small red silk baubles
3 Medium red silk baubles
3 Large red silk baubles
3 Large snow-tipped fir cones
9 Pieces of mistletoe
6 Stems of holly
1 Bird
1 Circle of Oasis foam for dried flowers
1 Large-diameter candle
Plasticine anchor
Oasis fix

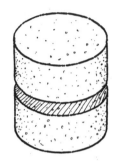

How it is made
Fix the plasticine anchor centrally on the board with Oasis fix. Cut the circle of Oasis foam in half horizontally so that it is 1½ inches deep. Put one of the halves centrally on the anchor.

Prepare the candle with 4 cocktail sticks securely fixed with sellotape and push onto the top of the foam (Fig. 1).

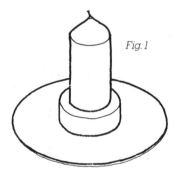

Fig. 1

Cut the white pine into pieces, each with 3 points, and fix each with a double-leg wire. Circle the board with white pine keeping the foliage flat and overlapping the board (Fig. 2).

Wire together one of each size of red bauble and make a stem with the wire. Push into the foam and position around these baubles, holly sprigs and mistletoe. Repeat this operation at two equi-distant positions around the circle.

Between these three points put a snow-tipped fir cone which has had a stem fixed with a double-leg wire.

Finally fill in any gaps with white pine foliage, especially between the candle and other material.

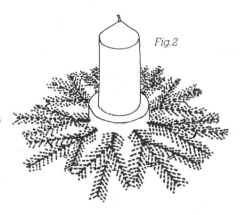

Fig. 2

 Variations
A gold chunky candle with old gold foliage and gold baubles will produce a warmer and richer look to this attractive arrangement.

Cool Carnations

This frosty winter scene of silver and white makes a startling contrast when set on a warm-coloured dresser or against a plain dark background.

The items you will need
1 Black wrought-iron scroll stand
7 White carnations
5 Silver apples
3 Stems silver eucalyptus foliage
3 Stems silver fern
6 Silver rose leaves
1 Stem glittered skeletonized leaves
1 Stem silver glittered conifer branches
1 Plasticine anchor
Oasis fix, Dri-Hard, Aluminium foil

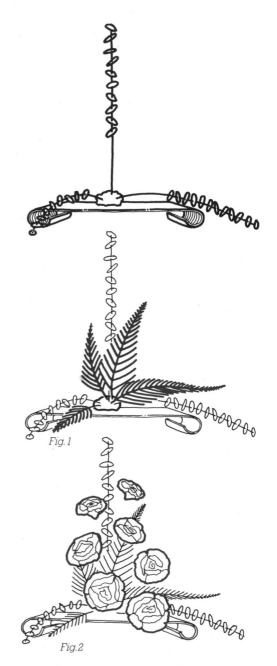

Fig. 1

Fig.2

How it is made
Stick the plasticine anchor to the left of centre on the scroll stand with Oasis fix. Make a ball of Dri-Hard, cover with aluminium foil and push onto the anchor.

Make the first three points of the triangle with pieces of eucalyptus foliage and then use silver fern leaves to amplify the points (Fig. 1).

Cut the carnation stems individually to length and position as shown in Figure 2.

Cut the glittered conifer branches into pieces and wire individually. Use to fill in. Do the same with the skeletonized foliage.

Use the large silver apples to complete the picture. Use the silver rose leaves and any remaining material to fill in wherever there is a gap or where you need to hide the mechanics of this arrangement.

 Variations
The same cool effect can be achieved if you use lemon carnations to provide a contrast to the black scroll base.

Silver Bell Outline

The delicate bell-shaped frame makes an attractive outline to contain a Christmas arrangement. Use in a hall or on a landing to give that special seasonal welcome.

The items you will need
1 Bell-shaped wire base
3 Stems of white flocked fern
4 Silver roses
10 Stems of small-leaved holly with berries
5 Yellow mini-carnations
4 Yards red picot ribbon
Plasticine, Aluminium foil

How it is made
This delicate arrangement has a definite face which is the traditional triangular shape. The topmost point of the triangle is set to the back and the base points are forward and lower than the base of the bell.

If the frame is bare metal, cover with fabric or metalized ribbon before you start. Suspend the bell in a convenient place so that you can arrange your material without strain.

Take a piece of plasticine, cover with aluminium foil and wire onto the centre of the base (Fig. 1).

Start with the three points of the triangle using white flocked fern. Cut the pieces to length so that the upright central point is within the confines of the bell shape (Fig. 2).

Now take the four silver roses and position as shown in Figure 3. Use holly to provide a contrast and to amplify the triangular outline you have created.

The yellow mini-carnations are scattered around the face of the arrangement to provide a light colour to this floral decoration. Hang long, looping bows to the base of the arrangement to hide the mechanics and top off with a largish 'figure of eight' bow.

Complete the arrangement using white flocked fern and holly foliage, making sure the back of the decoration is tidy and attractive.

 Variations
Cut the descending tail ribbons to varying lengths and stitch to each a small silver bauble.

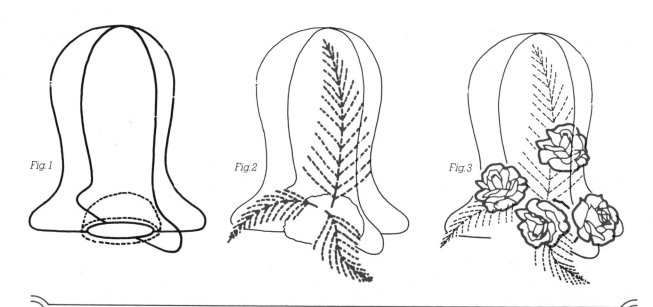

Fig. 1   Fig. 2   Fig. 3

Bambi Log

The natural bark base provides an interesting foundation to this woodland scene, complete with animal figure. Make sure that there will be no danger of scratching before positioning on a highly polished surface.

The items you will need
1 Piece of bark
7 Poinsettia flowers
9 Fir cones
3 Sprays of silver fern
3 Sprays of green pine
3 Yards of red ribbon
1 Bambi figure
1 Can of snow spray
Plasticine anchor
Oasis fix, Dri-Hard, Aluminium foil

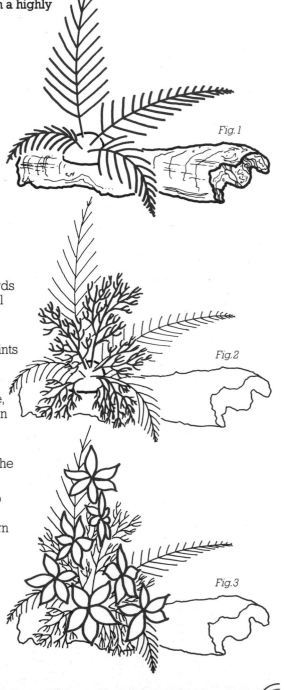

Fig. 1

Fig. 2

Fig. 3

How it is made

First spray the bark base with 'snow' to produce an interesting texture. Then stick the plasticine anchor towards the left hand end of the base using Oasis fix. Cover a small ball of Dri-Hard with aluminium foil and push onto the anchor.

Use pieces of silver fern to establish the four principle points of the arrangement (Fig. 1). Add pieces of pine foliage as shown in Figure 2, cutting each piece to the right length.

Position the poinsettia flowers to create a triangular shape, making sure each flower faces a slightly different direction (Fig. 3).

To fill in any obvious gaps use the pine cones which have been fixed to stout wires. The cones need to peep out of the arrangement without the wires being seen.

Three triple-loop bows made from red ribbon are used to complete the picture. Use two in the front of the arrangement. The remaining bow and off-cuts of silver fern or pine foliage are used to tidy up the back of the arrangement. Finally position the Bambi figure on the bark with Oasis fix.

Variations
Try glittery red fern, white poinsettias and the same snow-tipped pine foliage for an interesting change.

Fun-loving Santa

This is an ideal arrangement for the bedroom of any 'young-at-heart'.
The presents pouring out of Santa's sack is an exciting tantilizer for
the promise of Christmas Day.

The items you will need
1 Father Christmas container
3 Foil parcels on sticks
5 Pieces of holly
3 Mini-fir cones
2 White and gold bells
1 Small red cracker
Assorted foliage (green pine, red flocked fern, holly,
white flocked fern, silver fern)
1 Stem of gold icicles
1 Yard red spotted ribbon
Dri-Hard, Aluminium foil

Fig. 1

How it is made

Wrap sufficient Dri-Hard in aluminium foil to fill and overflow
the container. Push into the container.

Start by using green pine foliage to give three points as
shown in Figure 1. Cut and position these carefully, for these
will determine the height, width and depth of the
arrangement which must be in keeping with the size of the
Father Christmas figure.

Now use silver, red and white foliage to complete the outline
(Fig. 2).

The centre of the decoration is made up of holly foliage
and berries, some green fir and the mini-cones. Wire
the cracker and position behind the figure. Next come
the parcels, all pointing in a different direction.

The icicle is placed centrally and the two bells are wired
together and overhang at the front.

Finish off with triple-loop bows made from the spotted
ribbon (see Page 19).

 Variations
*There are other ceramic containers available which can
be used to create a similar effect. Small donkeys and
boots are available which can be used as an interesting
alternative.*

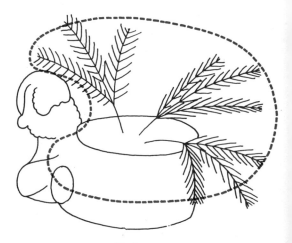

Fig. 2

Fireside Log

This simple fireside arrangement is different from most because of the use of tubular ribbon which can be bent to any shape required.

The items you will need
3 Silver glittered foliage spikes
3 Silk rose buds
2 Sprays of combined holly leaves, white pine fir and fir cones
1 Yard tubular red ribbon
1 Yard thick stub wire
1 Wood slice
Plasticine anchor
Oasis fix, Plasticine, Aluminium foil

Fig. 1

Fig. 2

Fig. 3

How it is made
Position the anchor in the middle of the wood slice using Oasis fix. Cover a ball of plasticine with aluminium foil and push onto the anchor.

Cut the tubular ribbon into 24 inch and 12 inch lengths and thread stub wire into each piece. Leave enough wire protruding from each end of the ribbon so that it can be turned back and then twisted around the ribbon for about one inch.

Bend the ribbons to shape and push the ends into the plasticine. In this arrangement we have pointed the tops to mirror the shape of the fireplace (Fig. 1) but you could make the ribbons circular if you prefer.

Cut the first silver spike so that it is just taller than the highest ribbon and position behind the two red hoops. The two other spikes are positioned at the front pointing in different directions. Now put in the three rose buds (Fig. 3).

Finally use the bunches of plastic foliage to fill in around the base. Cut the stems short so that the leaves hide all the aluminium foil.

Variations
Orange tubular ribbon could form the frame and yellow roses or carnations could provide the floral decoration.

Snow Scene

A snow scene for children to make is an exciting introduction to their Christmas – especially when there are sweets in store.

The items you will need
1 Square cake board or ceiling tile
1 Twig
1 Robin
1 Father Christmas
2 Reindeer
1 Aerosol can of snow flakes
7 Sweets
Plasticine anchor
1 Ball of Oasis foam, Oasis fix

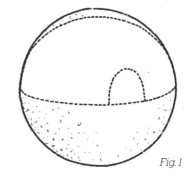

Fig. 1

How it is made
To make the igloo, simply cut the ball of Oasis in half and then shave off the top to make the correct shape. Cut out a door opening (Fig. 1).

Use Oasis fix plus plasticine anchor to fix the igloo to the board. Find a twig from the garden which resembles a miniature tree and position this to back left of the board using Oasis fix. The Father Christmas, robin and reindeer are stuck to the board using tiny blobs of the same material (Fig. 2).

When all are in position spray the arrangement with artificial snow flakes making sure the igloo is properly covered. Now tie the sweets onto the branches of the tree with cotton.

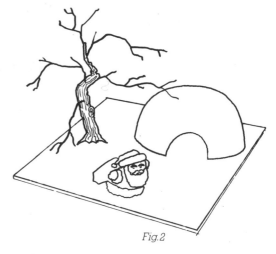

Fig.2

 Variations
Chocolate money is an obvious choice for the tree hangings. If the sweets disappear too quickly from the tree, replace with tiny baubles or miniature crackers.

Christmas Centrepiece

Where you have a long dining table this is the sort of arrangement
that fits in well and does not hinder conversation. By using plasticine
as a base, the candles can be replaced easily.

The items you will need
1 Long plastic dish
3 Slim red candles
6 Large red carnations
2 Large white carnations
8 Stems of white mini-carnations (5 per stem)
8 Stems of red mini-carnations (5 per stem)
3 Stems of green pine foliage
9 Pieces of small-leaved holly with berries
3 Yards red ribbon
2 Plasticine anchors
Oasis fix, Plasticine, Aluminium foil, Cocktail
sticks

How it is made
Fit the two anchors in the base of the dish with
Oasis fix. Roll the plasticine into a sausage shape,
wrap in aluminium foil and push onto the anchors
along the centre of the dish (Fig. 1).

Cut two of the candles slightly shorter than the
other one and prepare all of them with cocktail
sticks taped to their bases (see Page 15). Position

the tallest in the centre and the shorter ones either
side.

Now cover the edges of the dish using fir foliage
cut to length. Follow the plan in Figure 2 to
position the carnations, starting around the outside
and working towards the centre. You will find that
occasionally you will need to add more fir foliage
as a contrast in texture. Add the holly stems when
all the flowers are in position.

Finish off with double-loop bows scattered around
to fill in any gaps which may be apparent.

❄ Variations
*Match the candles and carnations to the colour
of your serviettes. You can
buy candles and
serviettes together
in matching shades.*

Fig. 1

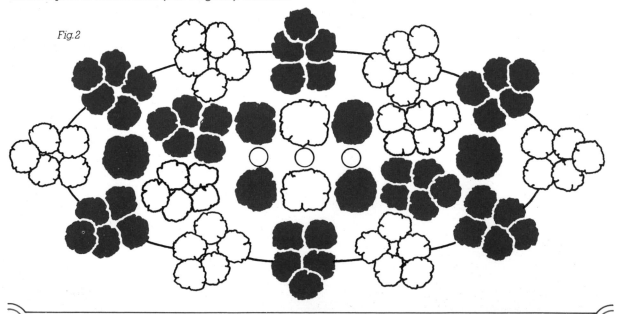

Fig. 2

Golden Hanging Swag

As an interesting alternative to the traditional door wreath this long
swag could be found a place in a living room or in a protected porch.
Use fine silver wire in this arrangement to make twisting easy and
less likely to show.

The items you will need
1 Golden cycas leaf
6 Golden baubles
2 Golden poinsettia flowers with foliage
1 Golden angel
2 Golden bells
1 Bunch of holly berries and fir cones
1 Yard golden ribbon
2 Yards green ribbon
Fine silver wire

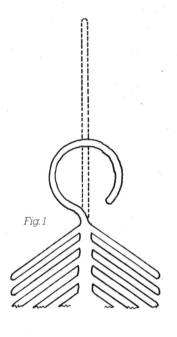

Fig.1

How it is made
Bend over the stem of the cycas leaf and use this as a hook (Fig.
1). Wire the top three golden baubles together and then push
the wire ends through to the back of the leaf and twist firmly
(Fig. 2). Cut off any excess wire.

The golden poinsettia flowers are usually only available with a
long thick stem so this must be cut down to ¼ inch (5mm)
before fixing. Use a double-leg silver wire to fix the poinsettia
flower to the central stem of the leaf, using the same method as
baubles.

Next wire the angel into position. Underneath the angel, wire
the second poinsettia flower and then three golden baubles.
Use the golden ribbon to make a single 'figure of eight' bow
and wire in the centre.

As a touch of colour to this arrangement use one bunch of holly
berries and fir cones. Now wire the two bells together and push
their tops under the foliage to hide the fixing.

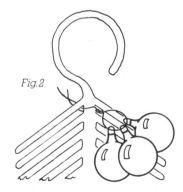

Fig.2

Finish off with a large green bow. We have used ¾ inch wide
ribbon to make a four-loop 'figure of eight' bow with long
descending tails cut to single points. Use a short piece of ribbon
to hide the centre wire of this bow which attaches it to the top of
the leaf.

 Variations
*Cycas leaves are available in silver to which you can wire a
mixture of silver and green material to become just as effective
a decoration. If you prefer a more colourful effect you can
introduce red poinsettias and brightly coloured baubles.*

Topiary Tree

This standard tree on a cane is very easy to arrange. The cane is fixed into an ordinary flower pot and is placed inside a decorative pot cover for its temporary time on display.

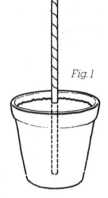

Fig. 1

The items you will need
1 Flower pot (3½ inches diameter)
1 Bamboo cane
1 Medium size sphere of Oasis for dried arrangements
8 Sprays of holly berries, pine needles and fir cone
6 Sprays holly with berries
16 Red baubles
4 Yards red decorette ribbon
Dri-Hard or Plaster of Paris
Decorative pot cover
Pot-topper pebbles

How it is made
Cut the bamboo cane to about 16 inches long and wrap with ribbon, using sticky tape at top and bottom to fix. Half fill the flower pot with Dri-Hard or wet plaster and position the cane in the pot centrally and upright (Fig. 1). Fill up with more Dri-Hard, and check vertical alignment. After waiting a day for the material to set, push the Oasis sphere onto the top of the cane.

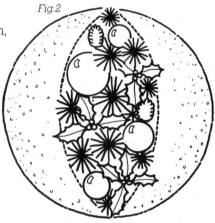

Fig. 2

Now cut the holly and pine clusters to about 1½ – 2 inches long. Each of these pieces will need to have a stem using a double-leg wire. The technique is shown on Page 12. The glass baubles should also be given a wire stem using the same method.

The easiest way to achieve an even cover of the sphere is to fill a quarter of the ball at one time. Start at the top and mix foliage and glass baubles as you go. Avoid placing similar material side by side (Fig. 2).

When the sphere is completely covered, take ribbon and wire three pieces so that the cut ends are all a different length. To add an exciting twist to the ribbon, run it between your thumb and the back of a knife. This gives a ringlet ribbon. Push the wire stems up into the Oasis at the base (Fig. 3).

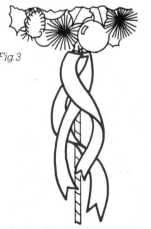

Fig. 3

Place the flower pot into a decorative pot cover and use expanded clay pebbles or Hortag Pot-Topper pebbles to fill in and cover.

 ### Variations
White silk Christmas roses make a good alternative to the red baubles and completely changes the look of the tree. Instead of a decorative pot cover you can wrap the basic plant pot with crepe paper or foil.

Pink Perfection

The arrangement pictured here mixes fresh variegated holly with the normal artificial material. By substituting plastic holly your arrangement will be everlasting and you will not have to remember to water it regularly.

The items you will need

1 Candlestick	7 Christmas roses
2 Pink candles	9 Pink mini-carnations
1 Large candle cup	9 Pinky/mauve glass baubles
1 Piece Oasis for fresh flowers	1 Fir cone
Fresh variegated holly	3 Yards silver decorette ribbon
3 Stems silver ivy leaves	Plasticine anchor
5 Stems silver maidenhair fern	Oasis, Oasis fix, Cocktail sticks

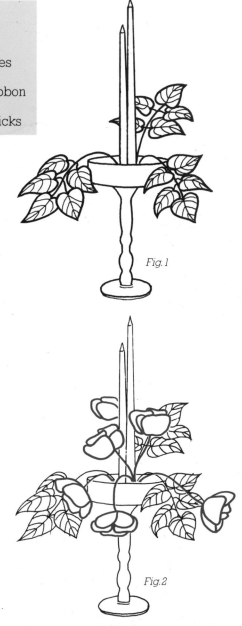

Fig. 1

Fig. 2

How it is made

Fit a candle cup to the candlestick and secure a plasticine anchor in the base with Oasis fix. After soaking thoroughly the piece of Oasis in water, push it firmly into the candle cup.

Cut one candle slightly shorter than the other one and then tape three pieces of cocktail stick to the base of each. Position the tallest candle centrally but to the back of the Oasis and the shorter one in front but slightly to the left.

Create the three points of the triangle using pieces of silver ivy (Fig. 1). Now position three Christmas roses along the base line of the triangle and three more pointing upwards around the candles (Fig. 2).

Use 5 pieces of silver maidenhair fern to complete the triangular shape. The centre of the arrangement is now filled with holly. Try to cut the pieces to the correct length before inserting them so that the Oasis remains intact.

Use the pink carnations and pink baubles to contrast the foliage and keep an overall triangular shape. The fir cone is wired next and positioned just to right of centre.

A large six-loop bow goes just above the cone and three double-loop bows are now prepared. Two go at the base and one is used at the back. Fill in the back with any left-over material.

 Variations
You can use white carnations as the floral theme of this arrangement and a bunch of plastic grapes in the centre to replace the fir cone.

Roses & Ribbons

Elegantly simple, this arrangement is ideally suited for a coffee table, sideboard or anywhere where the circular theme can be seen easily.

The items you will need
1 Circular white dish (approx. 5 inches diameter)
1 Red candle
3 Sprays gold fern
9 Clusters of holly berries, pine needles and fir cone
4 Large Christmas roses
4 Satin baubles
2 Yards red ribbon
Plasticine, Cocktail sticks, Aluminium foil

Fig. 1

How it is made

Take enough plasticine to make a ball and cover with aluminium foil. Push this ball into the base of the white dish firmly. Prepare the candle by taping three pieces of cocktail stick to the base as shown on Page 5. Position the candle dead centre and exactly vertical.

Cut the pieces of gold fern to length and encircle the dish (Fig. 1). Now take the small clusters of holly berries, pine needles and fir cone and cut them shorter than the gold fern. Place in a circle inside the gold fern. Now cut the stems of the Christmas roses to length and position just inside the greenery. The four satin baubles are usually filled with polystyrene and you can pierce them easily with a cocktail stick. Use the stick to position the baubles between the Christmas roses.

Make four triple-loop bows and position around the candle base to cover the mechanics.

Variations
Silver foliage contrasted with a blue candle, blue baubles and blue ribbons will give a cooler but more sophisticated look to the arrangement which may go well in certain room settings.

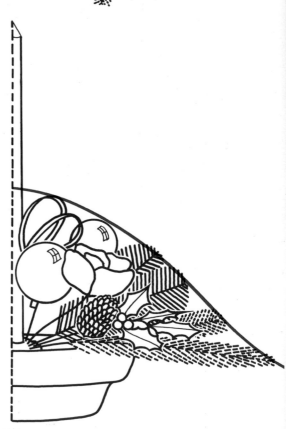

Ivy Pink

This attractive arrangement has been designed to sit at the end of a
mantlepiece. The ambitious will make two – one for either end.
Make sure they face towards each other.

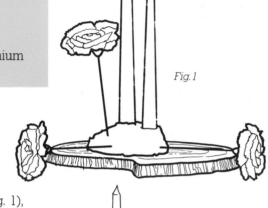
Fig.1

The items you will need
Small wood slice
2 Pink candles
13 Pink carnations
1 Large spray of polyester
begonia foliage

2 Sprays of polyester
variegated trailing ivy
2 Yards pink ribbon
Plasticine anchor
Plasticine, Oasis fix, Aluminium
foil, Cocktail sticks

How it is made
Stick the anchor to the wooden slice with Oasis fix at a
position one third from the left hand edge. Push on a
large ball of plasticine wrapped in aluminium foil.
Tape cocktail sticks to the candles and position slightly
apart but truly vertical.

Make the three points of a triangle with pink carnations (Fig. 1),
making sure the base flowers overlap the edges of the wood slice.

Use begonia and ivy leaves to amplify these base points making sure
they will sit on the mantlepiece and not fly upwards in mid-air (Fig. 2).
If there are any begonia leaves over, use individually to
cover the ball of plasticine.

Position the other carnations to complete the soft triangle
as pictured.

Now provide an interesting edge to the triangular shape with
variegated ivy. The stems and leaves will need a double-leg
wire covered with green stem wrap for a perfect finish.
Individual leaves can be wired and covered and then positioned
to give an interesting contrast between individual flowers.

Make a triple-loop bow and wire into position centrally.
Now make a triple-point ribbon piece and
position below the triple-loop bow.

Fig.2

Variations
*If you make a pair, visually and
physically join them together
with a delicate trail of ivy leaves*

Hearth-side Pixie

Arrangements don't have to be big to be beautiful. You can add a festive feel to a fireplace using artificial material arranged in a container the size of an egg cup.

The items you will need
1 Small vase or egg cup
5 Red glittered bulrushes
4 Stems of small poinsettia flowers (3 blooms per stem)
5 Stems polyester holly foliage (2 sprays per stem)
3 Pine cones
1 Yard silver decorette ribbon
Dri-Hard, Aluminium foil

How it is made

Take enough Dri-Hard to fill and overflow the container, wrap in aluminium foil and push firmly into place.

Cut the bulrushes to length and position as shown in Figure 1. Wire three pieces of holly and bend the stems so that these pieces can fall below the top level of the vase (Fig. 2). Now go around the rim of the vase alternating a piece of holly with a poinsettia flower. For the vase illustrated, 5 pieces of each were needed.

Wire the fir cones and position close to the base of the bulrushes.

Position the remaining poinsettia blooms to fill the centre section of the arrangement.

Finish off with three double-loop bows of silver decorette ribbon pushed in close to the base.

 Variations
Instead of red poinsettias try golden glittered roses.

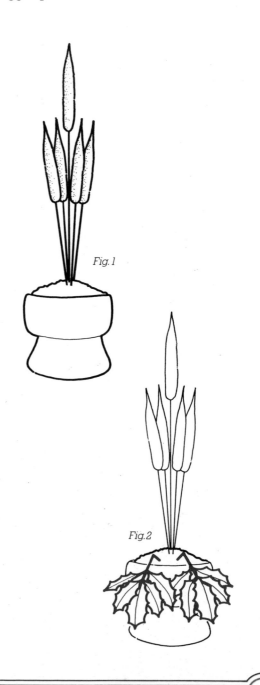

Fig. 1

Fig. 2

Brandy Candle

This versatile design can be used on coffee tables or can be used in the centre of a buffet table to add a touch of luxury.

The items you will need
1 Oval wood slice
6 Pieces of glittered silver fern
6 Stems of silver boxwood (4 pieces per stem)
2 Yards orange ribbon
1 Orange candle
Plasticine anchor
Plasticine, Oasis fix, Cocktail sticks,
Aluminium foil

How it is made
Use an anchor positioned with Oasis fix to hold a small ball of plasticine covered with aluminium foil. Prepare the candle with cocktail sticks taped to the base and position centrally. Cut down the silver fern leaves in proportion to the wood slice base and use these to radiate from the centre (Fig. 1). Five points are usually sufficient. Use the remaining leaf and the pieces removed from the other stems to complete a circle smaller than the original one, and raised slightly from the base (Fig. 2).

Use the silver boxwood cut to length to fill in between the candle and the outer leaves.

Make four double-loop bows with the ribbon and position these evenly around the arrangement.

 ### Variations
Any colour candle with matching ribbon would look attractive in this basically silver arrangement. Dark green or purple are good colours to try, especially if you can find sweets or other accessories to match.

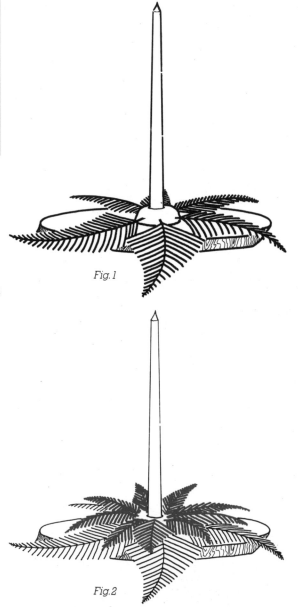

Fig. 1

Fig.2

The Long Boat

At night, this arrangement with candles aglow is great for leaving at a window without net curtains.

The items you will need
1 Boat-shaped container
3 Red candles
3 Sprays green pine foliage
15 Red carnations
8 Silver bells
4 Yards red ribbon
3 Plasticine anchors
Plasticine, Oasis fix, Aluminium foil, Cocktail sticks

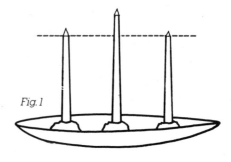

Fig. 1

How it is made
Position the first anchor centrally using Oasis fix. The other two are positioned half-way between the central point and each end of the boat.

Take three balls of plasticine and wrap each in aluminium foil. Push these onto the anchors. Tape securely three pieces of cocktail sticks to the base of each candle. Push these candles into the plasticine, the tallest one in the centre. Make sure the candles are upright from all angles (Fig. 1).

The sprays of green pine should be cut down to pieces 4 inches long, each wired securely with a double-leg wire.

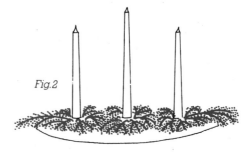

Fig.2

Cover the rim of the boat all the way round by pushing pieces of pine foliage horizontally into the plasticine so that they overlap the edge. Fill in the centre of the boat with foliage, making sure the base of each candle is covered (Fig. 2).

Cut the carnation stems to length and position as shown in Figure 3. Wire the silver bells in pairs using a double-leg wire, and push in evenly around the arrangement. Finish off with eight double-loop bows, four on each side.

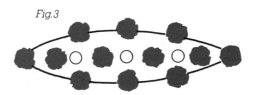

Fig.3

 Variations
A pink theme is almost as festive. Make sure that when selecting your candles and carnations the colours match each other.

Toadstool Log

Colourful woodland toadstools lift this arrangement out of the ordinary and can be easily purchased. The winter scene can be completed with artificial snow spray.

The items you will need
1 Small wood slice
1 Tree log (approx. 4 inches diameter)
4 Large toadstools
3 Small toadstools
1 Feathered robin
1 Red candle
1 Spray long-needled pine foliage
1 Spray snow-edged fir foliage
7 Twigs of holly with berries
5 Pieces of mistletoe
2 Yards red ribbon
Plasticine, Oasis fix, Aluminium foil,
Cocktail sticks

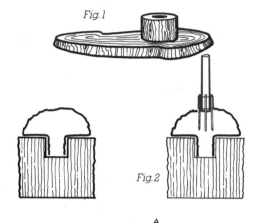

Fig. 1

Fig. 2

How it is made
Position the log one third from the right hand edge of the wood slice and stick together using several small pieces of Oasis fix (Fig. 1). Take enough plasticine to make a small ball and wrap in aluminium foil. Push the base of this ball into the hole in the tree log (Fig. 2). Tape cocktail sticks to the base of the candle and position centrally in the plasticine.

Start arranging the foliage material with three pieces of long-needled pine cut to length and positioned as shown in Figure 3. Now use the snow-edged fir cut to length and fill the positions shown in Figure 4. Use any pieces left over to fill in at the back.

Use three pieces of mistletoe at the front and two at the back and then position the holly pieces. Each piece will need to be wired with a double-leg wire and the stem cut to length.

So that the pretty robin sits happily in the arrangement you will need to wire each leg separately. Cut the wire stems to length so that the robin looks as if it is sitting on a branch and not suspended in mid-air.

Make five double-looped bows and use to fill in any gaps. Complete the base by positioning the toadstools using small pieces of Oasis fix.

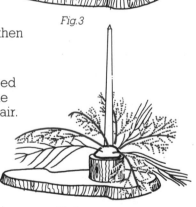

Fig. 3

Fig. 4

Variations
Try other woodland animals including squirrels, mice and birds. Make sure that they are in proportion to the arrangement and do not dominate too much.

Ice Blue Curves

Instead of the normal red and green arrangement, here is an all-blue idea. This looks particularly attractive against a plain wall in a room with matching hues.

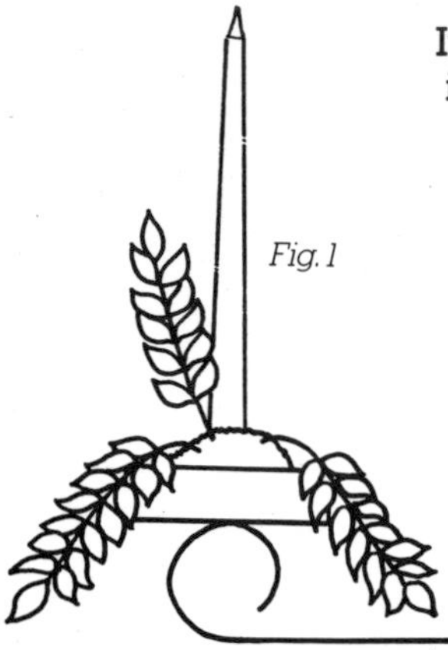

Fig. 1

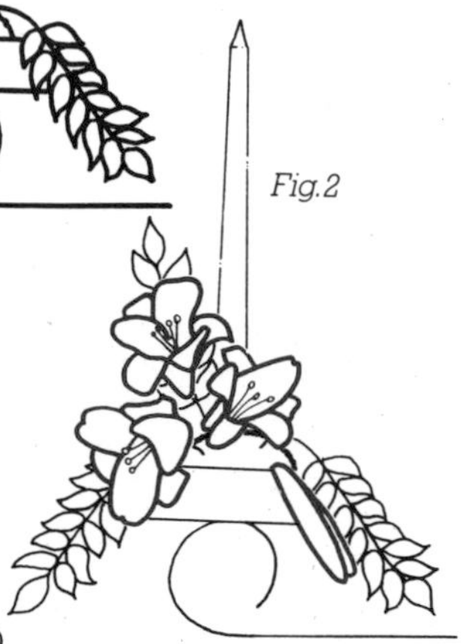

Fig. 2

Fig. 3

Fig. 4

The items you will need

Black wrought iron container with two levels
3 Sprays of polyester pale blue lily flowers
7 Polyester dark blue roses (open)
3 Polyester dark blue roses (buds)
4 Stems of dark blue single azalea flowers
7 Stems of silver icicles each 4 spires per stem
3 Stems of silver skeletonized leaves
5 Stems silver ruscus foliage
2 Blue candles
2 Plasticine anchors
Plasticine, Oasis fix, Aluminium foil, Cocktail sticks

How it is made

Start at the bottom level by positioning an anchor with Oasis fix in the centre of the holder. Make a ball of plasticine, cover with aluminium foil and push onto the prongs of the anchor.

Prepare the candles with pieces of cocktail stick taped to their base and push vertically and centrally into the plasticine. Start the arrangement with the first three points using silver ruscus foliage cut and bent to shape (Fig. 1). Amplify these points with pale blue lily flowers (Fig. 2). Use rose flowers and azaleas to fill in the centre (Fig. 3). Silver skeletonized leaves are positioned to contrast the dark blue roses and silver icicles are used to soften the top line at both sides of the candle.

Now start on the top arrangement with the candle fixed centrally using an anchor and plasticine. Take stems of light blue lily, cut and bend to shape to fill the positions shown in Figure 4. Azalea flowers and blue roses fill in the centre and emphasise the soft S-shaped line which you are trying to achieve.

Use more lily flowers in the centre to contrast the dark blue roses. Fill in with silver icicles and skeletonized silver leaves, making sure the back of the arrangement is full and the mechanics covered.

 Variations
Shades of cerise pink flowers with silver candles are stunning. You should keep within one colour range however to maintain the right effect.

Circular Garland

This traditional design is always popular and is simple to make.

The items you will need
3 Stems of pine foliage
4 Stems variegated holly
3 Snow-tipped pine cones
3 Christmas roses
2 Yards red ribbon
1 Circular wire frame
   Moss, wire

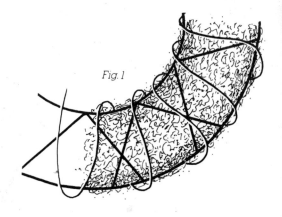

Fig. 1

How it is made
Use mossing wire or string to attach the moss to the face of the circular wire frame.

Cut up the stems of pine foliage and holly into small pieces and add a double-leg wire to each.

Fill the outer edge of the circle with pine foliage coming out at an angle like flares from a catherine wheel (Fig. 2). Do the same on the inside of the circle. Now fill the face with holly foliage. Push the wire stems right through the moss and bend them back on themselves so that the foliage is secure but there are no ends of wire to scratch paintwork.

At the base of the circle add the three Christmas roses and surround with the three pine cones.

Finish off with a double-loop bow wired under the flowers and two long ribbon tails cut to points.

Check that no wire ends are sticking out at the back or they will scratch the door.

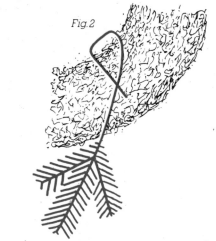

Fig. 2

Variations
If you have a laurel bush in the garden these dark glossy leaves give an excellent covering to the mossed frame.

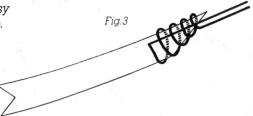

Fig. 3

Partridge in a Pear Tree

This nesting bird on a large piece of bark is easy to make and pleasing to the eye. It can be used on a windowsill or as an unobtrusive table centre.

The items you will need
1 Piece of bark
5 Pieces of holly with berries
7 Pieces of short-needled pine
1 Large bird
1 Can of snow spray
Plasticine anchor
Oasis fix, Dri-Hard, Aluminium foil

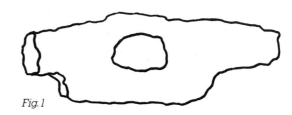
Fig. 1

How it is made

First spray the bark with 'snow' to produce an interesting texture. Then stick the plasticine anchor in the centre of the bark using Oasis fix. Cover a small ball of Dri-Hard with aluminium foil and push onto the anchor (Fig. 1).

Cut the pine needle sprays down to three-headed pieces and secure each piece with a double-leg wire. Push in the pine foliage to form a circle using about seven pieces. The pine foliage should be positioned close to the bark at the front of the arrangement (Fig. 2). Next add colour with the holly berries and leaves, the stems of which should be cut much shorter than the pine foliage (Fig. 3).

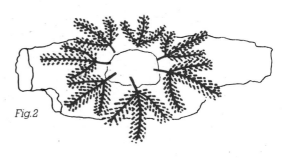
Fig. 2

Arrange the holly in a circular shape hiding most of the aluminium foil.

Now add wire stems to the legs of the bird and position in the centre of the arrangement. Try to position the bird close to the foliage so that it is seen to be nesting and not flying through the air.

 Variations
Variegated holly and white glittered pine would add sparkle to the arrangement but you should omit the snow spray or there will be little contrast between the sprayed bark and the light coloured foliage.

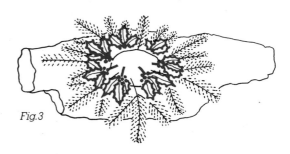
Fig. 3

Hanging Lantern

This hanging arrangement would look lovely in a window, especially if
it can be illuminated at night.

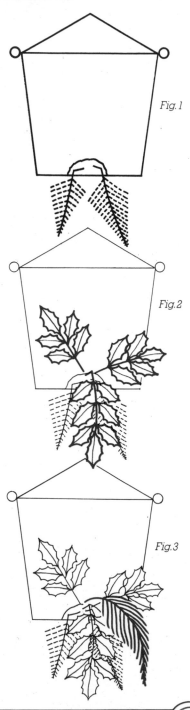

Fig. 1

Fig. 2

Fig. 3

The items you will need

1 White wire lantern base	4 Stems of gold glittered holly
5 Red glittered bulrushes	4 Gold plated fern leaves
4 Large poinsettia blooms	3 Gold bells
4 Stems of small poinsettia blooms (3 per stem)	4 Yards of red ribbon
	Plasticine anchor
6 Stems of large green holly	Oasis fix, Dri-Hard,
6 Pieces of white flocked fern	Aluminium foil

How it is made

In the base of the lantern place a ball of Dri-Hard covered with
aluminium foil using a plasticine anchor and Oasis fix. Hang the lantern
at a convenient height so that the material can fall over the edges
without twisting.

If you treat each of the four panels as a separate arrangement this will
help to keep your material organised. The description which follows is
for one panel but you should repeat each step for all panels as you go
along.

Cut each of the gold ferns into two pieces, bend the stems to almost
right angles (Fig. 1), and position to overhang the base. Now position
holly in each panel. One piece should trail down, one piece be just
above the base facing out and the last piece pointing upwards (Fig. 2).

Now position the white flocked fern so that it comes trailing
downwards from the bottom right hand corner (Fig. 3). Now that the
trailing pieces are in position you can start on the centre.

Cut to length the red glittered bulrushes. The tallest one in the centre
should go into the top part of the lantern. The other four are positioned
centrally in each panel. Cut some holly pieces very short and position
to hide some of the foil. Position the four large poinsettias facing
upwards. Use the gold glittered holly cut short to fill in around the top
and to add some sparkle to the arrangement. Use four small poinsettia
flowers to fill in any gaps.

Make a triple loop bow for each panel and three or four ribbon tails.
Position as shown in the photograph. To complete the arrangement,
thread the bells onto ribbon and tie each to a different length. Wire the
ribbon loop to the underside base of the lantern.

 Variations
*The centre bull rush stem can be replaced with a sculptured
candle, although because it will be close to the material it is safer
not to light it.*

Mirror Topper

This unusual but highly attractive decoration adds a festive touch to any mirror. It is especially useful in a hall where it will be seen by all your incoming guests.

The items you will need
2 Long stems of polyester ivy foliage
2 Short stems of polyester ivy foliage
3 Stems of snow tipped plastic pine foliage
6 Stems of artificial pine/holly and cone
2 Large plastic Christmas roses
1 Pine cone
3 Large gold baubles
3 Yards gold ribbon
Wires, stem wrap

How it is made
This arrangement is made in two separate sections – the horizontal run along the top and the trailing left hand piece. When both are completed they are joined together to fit the mirror.

Cut off the long thick stems from any material and add a short thin wire to these pieces and the gold baubles. Cover the individual wires with stem wrap.

To make the top run, take a long stem of ivy foliage and at the base where the leaves finish use stem wrap to fix a piece of pine, holly and cone (Fig. 1). Do not cut any stems and avoid twisting one stem around the other. Simply lay the foliage along the stem of the previous piece and wrap with binding tape. Add two more pieces of this mixed foliage.

Now add a wired gold bauble making sure the stem is securely in place.

A Christmas rose and the large pine foliage are next wrapped into position. See that the arrangement gets wider the further down the stem you work and use another bauble and a piece of ivy foliage to achieve this.

For the second piece use the same technique. Take a piece of ivy foliage and use stem wrap to attach pieces onto the stem. Start with a mixed foliage piece followed by a bauble and a bow. Keep this second piece narrow.

You can now join the two pieces together. Bend the stem of each piece so that they fall into position to frame your mirror, (Fig. 2), and wire together with fine silver wire. Fill in the gap between the pieces with a Christmas rose, a gold bauble and a double tail of ribbon. Wrap all the stems with stem wrap to protect the wall and mirror frame from damage.

 Variations
Choose the colour of baubles and ribbon to match the frame of your mirror, or the main colour of the room. Silver is an obvious choice, but if this is chosen change the white Christmas roses to red carnations.

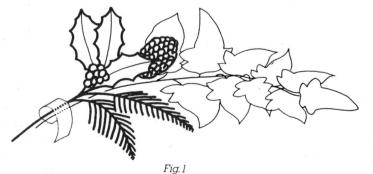

Fig. 1

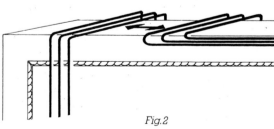

Fig. 2

Sleigh Ride

This delightful arrangement uses as its base an attractive wire sleigh shape.
The triangular shaped design carries a Father Christmas and much glittering material.

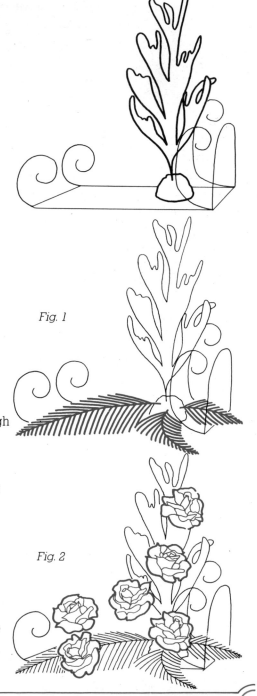

Fig. 1

Fig. 2

The items you will need
1 Wrought iron wire sleigh with solid platform base
1 Piece of golden stag's horn fern leaf
1 Father Christmas figure
6 Green shimmer silk roses
3 Snow-tipped plastic pine cones
9 Gold-glittered bulrushes
3 Green-glittered leaves
3 Gold-plated fern leaves
7 Gold-glittered baubles on sticks
1 Piece of silk holly with berries
3 Yards ½" red ribbon
Plasticine anchor
Oasis fix, Dri-Hard, Aluminium foil

How it is made
Fix a plasticine anchor to the metal base of the sleigh with
Oasis fix. Cover a ball of Dri-Hard with aluminium foil and
push onto the anchor.

Start with the tallest piece of stag's horn fern to give height to
the arrangement. Use the pieces of gold bracken to form the
base, cutting back the stems so that the points do not overlap
the sleigh too far (Fig. 1).

Now cut the 6 silk roses to length so that they strengthen the
triangular shape and position at the points shown in Figure 2.
The green-glittered leaves are cut and positioned next,
followed by Father Christmas who goes to the back of the sleigh

Wire the three cones and position to the centre and at the
base of the arrangement. Add the golden bulrushes all cut to
different lengths. Fill in any bare spots with silk holly. Last of
the solid materials are the golden baubles some of which go at
the back of the sleigh.

Finally make two double-loop bows from the ribbon and wire
in position at the back and to the left. Now make three ribbon
tails and turn into ringlet shapes by running the ribbon
between your thumb and the back of a knife. Fix at the front
right to balance the loop bows.

 Variations
*White carnations instead of gold roses would emphasise
the shape of the arrangement and would contrast well
against dark green foliage instead of the gold leaves.*

Finishing off

To complete any arrangement it is always worthwhile viewing it from all angles to check that there are no unsightly sides. Here is an arrangement which at the back reveals all the mechanics of stems and aluminium foil base. It will pay dividends if this is disguised so that the arrangement can be viewed from any angle.

Find some foliage, odd flowers or some spare ribbon and add wire stems to each. Covering the wires with stem-wrap will improve the appearance. Now use three of the pieces with longish stems to make a triangle.

Continue to fill in at the base, working towards the centre. Finish off with a flower or a ribbon. On the right you can see the back of the completed arrangement. When finished off in this manner the decoration can be placed in any position.

The Front

The Back

Bases for display

Many arrangements are created in tiny saucers, dishes or even lids from coffee jars. Most are completely hidden by the foliage and flowers and need not be disguised. You may find however that a decorative base which is matched to the colour and shape of the arrangement will enhance its appearance.

Bases can be made from all manner of materials. They can be bought ready made as cake bases, table mats or cork sections. Making your own is possible with thick cardboard, a polystyrene ceiling tile or wood. Covering these utility bases with fabric is easy and worthwhile. Choose your material to emphasise the colouring in the arrangements.

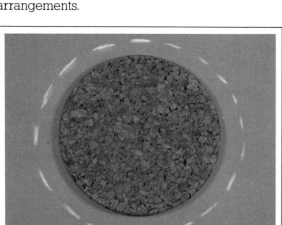

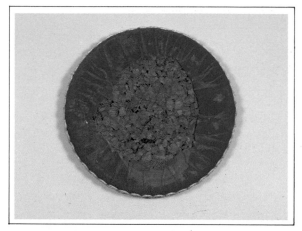

Cork Bases
Place the chosen base on the reverse side of the fabric material. Mark a circle large enough to give enough material to cover the sides and overlap the underneath by 1 inch. Cut out the material.

Replace the base onto the reverse of the material and glue into position. A few pins will hold the material taught while the glue dries.

Finish off with a decorative edging glued to the sides, if it is deep enough.

Bases don't have to be circular – oval, rectangular or free-style shapes are all possible with a steady hand or a handy meat dish or plate to give you the right shape.

Pub Drip Mats

These cardboard bases can be covered with silver paper and an arrangement created for one of the corners. In the example here the stems must be wired finely and the base of plasticine must be small enough to be covered by the material. If you have the time, a place setting for each dinner guest with matching napkin decoration is a delightful idea.

Napkins

If you have napkin rings they can be decorated with a tiny arrangement to compliment your table centre. Alternatively, fold the napkin to make a pocket and slip a corsage arrangement into the top.

Budget bases

Although the simple saucers and containers available in florists or garden centres are inexpensive you may like to make your own.

The lid from a coffee jar can be covered with aluminium foil to give a useful holder of a foam circle, so will the top from a can of spray paint. When you have finished the bottle of washing-up liquid you can cut off the bottom to give another useful container. It is not unknown for empty cans of Baked Beans to do duty as containers once they have been painted. You may find that rubbing the surface with sandpaper and giving it an undercoat of matt emulsion will give a better surface to take the spray paint.

Larger still is the use of a flower pot, either painted or covered with string or twine. Simply wind it round and round from the top down. Glue will keep the string in place.

From the kitchen, a wine glass can easily be used for the smaller arrangements which need to be lifted off the base.

A wine bottle can also be pressed into service with the use of a candle cup fixed into the neck. Green or brown bottles are more often favoured rather than the clear ones.

The circular wire frame used by florists as the basis of a door garland can be replaced with a wire coat hanger. Simply pull it into shape and tie moss onto the wire until it is well padded.

Budget materials

You can collect plenty of materials from gardens and hedgerows which can be used successfully in Christmas flower arrangements.

Foliage which has been preserved with glycerine during the summer can be pressed into use. Here the mahonia, beech, magnolia, *Choisya*, ferns, whitebeam, laurel and ivy are most commonly preserved. All can be coloured with a can of spray paint. Some will take the colour easily, others will just hold a highlighting tint. To turn the glycerined material from brown to white simply hang the material outside so that it can be bleached by the sun.

There are many seedheads which can be air dried and later sprayed with paint. Teasel, iris, love-in-a-mist, honesty, lavender, poppy and the Chinese lantern are good examples. So, of course, are beech nut cases and pine cones.

Flower heads too can be grown for drying and winter use. The everlasting flower (*Helichrysum*) and *Statice* are most popular and so are the yellow heads of *Achillea*. Sea lavender, delphinium, *Acroclinium* and *Rhodanthe* are also very suitable. Gather these flowers on a dry day before they are in full flower. Tie them together in bundles and hang them upside down in a dry garage or a dark cupboard.

Seeds themselves can be used. The acorn or the walnut can be used in their natural state or they can be sprayed with paint. Insert a wire into the acorn while it is still green.

Indexes

Visual Index

Page 22

Page 24

Page 26

Page 28

Page 38

Page 40

Page 42

Page 44

Page 54

Page 56

Page 58

Page 60

Page 70

Page 72

Page 74

Page 76

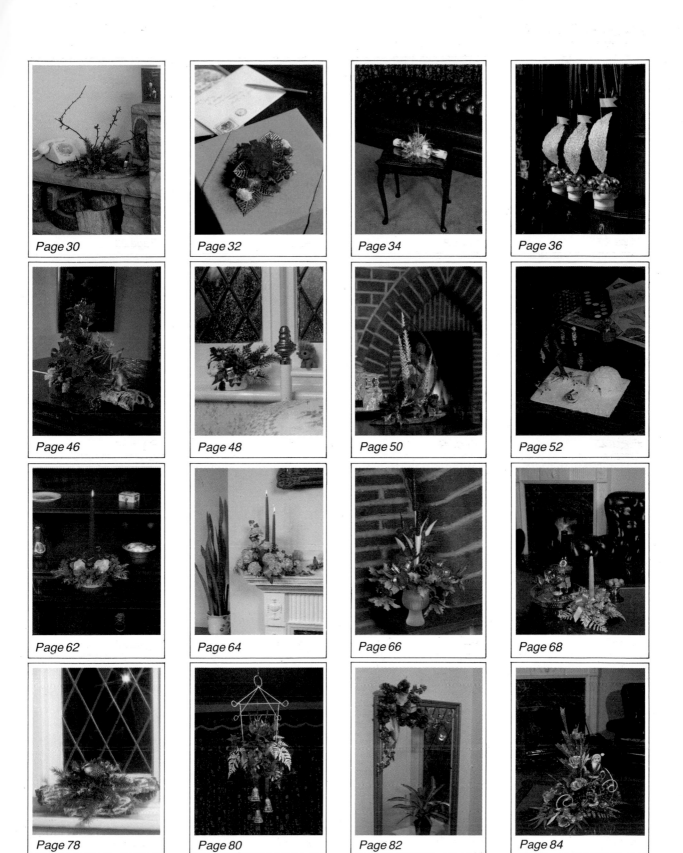

Index